IMAGES OF ENGLAND

CULLERCOATS

IMAGES OF ENGLAND

CULLERCOATS

RAY MARSHALL

TEMPUS

Frontispiece: A Cullercoats lifeboat man tries to get a line aboard a stricken ship heading for the rocks.

First published 2007

Tempus Publishing
Cirencester Road, Chalford,
Stroud, Gloucestershire, GL6 8PE
www.tempus-publishing.com

Tempus Publishing is an imprint of NPI Media Group

British Library Cataloguing in Publication Data.
A catalogue record for this book is available from the British Library.

ISBN 978 0 7524 4285 3

Typesetting and origination by NPI Media Group
Printed in Great Britain

Contents

Three of the fishwives so revered by the American artist Winslow Homer. The real women pictured here are every bit as lovely as those portrayed in Winslow's paintings.

Introduction

The name of Cullercoats brings to mind the old world charm of the fishing communities that once flourished for centuries around our coasts. But, compared with its near neighbours, Cullercoats is fairly young, an infant in fact according to William Weaver Tomlinson, who published the famous *Tomlinson's Comprehensive Guide To Northumberland* in 1888. He estimated its age at the time as a mere 300 years.

Originally it was called Arnold's Close, with a water mill, steaming salt pans and a handful of cottages. In fact, the town probably owes its birth more to the salt pans than the fishing folk. In the early days and mainly because of the salt pans and its proximity to the Whitley collieries it became a prosperous little port. Ships would arrive in the little harbour and load up with salt and coal brought in on the waggonway and grindstones.

According to Tomlinson the last clearance from the port of Cullercoats was *The Fortune of Whitby*, on 18 July 1726, with a cargo of 21 tons of salt. Records show that in the Michaelmas quarter of 1723, 1,962 tons of salt were exported from Cullercoats. But today we only associate Cullercoats with the men of the cobles and the ladies of the creels who sustained it through later years and brought it recognition. The men and their cobles, the graceful little sail-driven fishing boats, fighting the harsh elements and deadly storms which the North Sea can whip up at a moment's notice and the brown-faced fisherwomen, with their petticoats billowing as they traversed the North-East towns selling their men's catch and, obviously, carrying the strong smell of fish.

Surprisingly, an artists' community grew up in Cullercoats which was frequented by such well-known painters as H.H. Emmerson, Birket, Foster and J.D. Watson. But it was the great American painter Winslow Homer who drew most interest and it was here that he entered the most productive and defining part of his career, especially with his paintings of the fisherwomen who he obviously came to adore. Cullercoats may have been classed as a small village, but four important buildings stand out above all others in this community: the Watch House from where the lifeboat was launched, Sparrow Hall, Cliff House and the Fishermen's Mission.

For obvious reasons the lifeboat was one of the great mainstays of the Cullercoats community, crewed by volunteers who were willing to gamble with their lives as they battled mountainous seas to come to the aid of ships in distress or local fishermen caught in one of the many tempests which frequently engulf our coastline. Although the Cullercoats Volunteer Life Brigade was established in 1865 there had already been in existence a Cullercoats lifeboat and crew. Records show that both lifeboats were called out on 3 June 1897 when the *Luna*, laden with timber for Newcastle, came ashore on Half Moon Rocks and was dashed to pieces on Whitley beach.

What proved an interesting sidenote to the event was that according to reports of the North Shields magistrates' court, a Philip Taylor from Cullercoats and two other men were crabbing when they came across the *Luna*. Returning to the town they raised the alarm then boarded the Cullercoats lifeboat and put on lifebelts ready to help with any rescue. But they were stopped by the deputy coxswain along with another fisherman, Robert Arthur, who insisted the lifeboat only go out with its proper crew. When the lifeboat returned Philip Taylor was waiting on the beach and confronted Robert Arthur who was injured in a stand-up fight.

Robert Arthur's mother, Isabella Mason, tried to interfere and was knocked down trying to separate them. Isabella was seen throwing stones at Philip Taylor and his brother John. The episode ended with John and Philip Taylor being fined 20s or given the option of a month in prison.

The village is full of famous stories of catches and rescues and also families such as the Lisles and the Jeffersons but today no one is better remembered than fisherwoman Polly Donkin. Polly made her name not with the fish which she sold over many years, but in travelling the North East in a traditional fishwife's costume, raising money for the lifeboats. Polly, born in 1858, worked as a fishwife until the age of seventy, but was an active collector until she died in 1951.

Today no cobles venture out from Cullercoats and the lifeboat station lies empty. But if you stand by the Watch House you can still imagine the hustle and bustle of the cobles being made ready for sea and the lines being baited by the fisherwomen, ready for their men to do battle once again with the North Sea, to earn their keep.

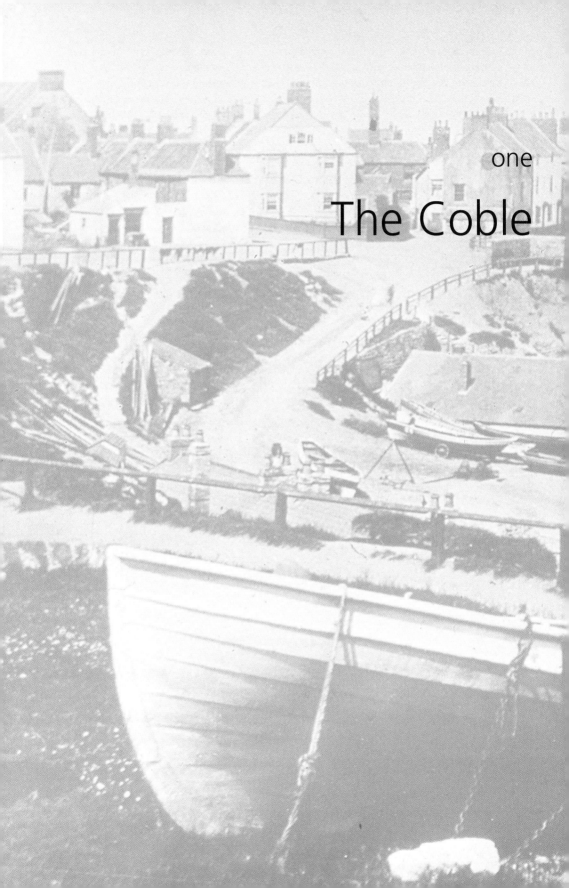

one

The Coble

It is known that by 1880, there were eighty fishing cobles based in Cullercoats harbour and the open area to the south of the bay was known as the Boat Field. It was here that the fishermen hauled their boats from the sea during bad weather and set out their nets and gear ready for repair. Most of the cobles were produced at Hartlepool by the firm of Cambridge Bros. The cobles were painted a variety of colours, the usual combinations being blue and white, blue and green or pink, and black and white. They were clinker built, using larch, about 27 to 32ft long and 6 to 8ft in the beam; open boats of graceful outline. Flat-bottomed with two bilge keels running fore and aft about 2ft apart, often made of oak then shod with iron like two deep sledge runners, they were designed for running in and beaching. Because of their size they offered seasonal versatility so that the fishermen could fish long-line from October to February, then work the lobster pots until May, then drift for herring with nets. On the service boards in the lifeboat house at Cullercoats, many of the entries in the nineteenth and early part of the twentieth centuries state, 'Gave aid to fishing cobles'. An interesting feature of the bows of the coble is the deep and sharp forefoot which has developed. This is invaluable in beaching the boats stern-first.

Coble owners were often pilots for the River Tyne, who would make their way south to the Yorkshire coast to find a ship in need of their services. The coble would then be towed stern-first and the deep bow acted as a fixed rudder and prevented the coble yawing behind the towing vessel. Towing a coble bow-first, when the rudder is damaged or missing, is an invitation for trouble, since the fore-foot then acts as a rudder and will flip the coble over quite quickly.

Cullercoats Bay takes shape. Above and below are artist's impressions of how the small fishing village evolved through the 1800s.

Fishermen work on their cobles and nets.

The bay pictured around the late 1800s. The cobles lie on the beach ready for sea.

Day trippers mingle with the fishermen as they prepare their nets in 1900.

Cullercoats fishermen prepare to push their coble away from the harbour wall.

A group of fishwives, some washing the fish, some awaiting the return of the cobles with their catch.

Motor-driven cobles, strung together to save fuel, head for the shore after a day's fishing in the 1930s.

A group of young lads enjoy a rest on the side of the lifeboat.

Andrew Taylor was coxswain on the lifeboat *Co-operator No. 1* in 1884. The lifeboat, as the name suggests, was donated by the Co-operative Society.

Lifeboat crew pose in the *Co-operator No. 1* before they go on a training exercise.

With oars raised high, in full drill form, the crew of *Co-operator 2*, ready for launch.

Cullercoats Fisherwomen

These pages: The Jefferson family. On the page opposite is a Jefferson fisherman with his children, showing off the pride of the day's catch. Above, two more Jeffersons prepare the crabs for cooking. Below, George, watched by members of the family, prepares the lobster pots ready for laying. The fisherman on the right is holding a lobster.

Brown's buildings in Cullercoats. The fishwives have cleaned the barrels and creels ready for when the cobles return.

A quiet day in Cullercoats as a horse trots down Bank Top pulling its cab.

Belle Wilson and Nannie Gallon are among the passengers on this fish wagon.

Fish, crabs, lobsters and winkles are put on display and sold from the fishermen's cottages.

Members of the Jefferson family standing outside their Cullercoats home.

A Cullercoats fisherwoman, Mrs McCulley, sells fresh crab on her stall.

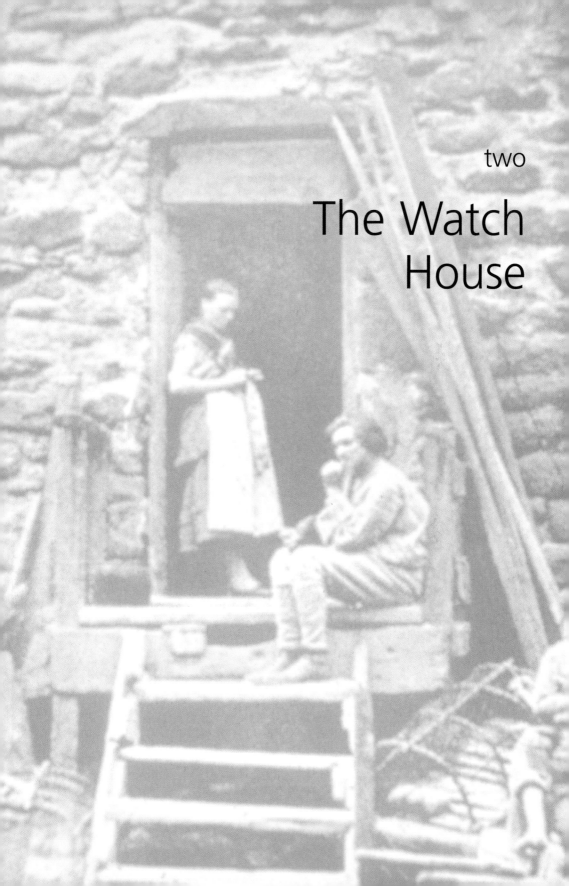

two

The Watch House

For many years, when the weather was bad and danger lurked out at sea, the fisherfolk of Cullercoats used to gather together under the lee of an old wall to watch for the returning cobles bringing their husbands, fathers, sons and brothers, with their catches, back to the safety of the little harbour.

It was decided, around 1877, to erect a building to house the lifeboat for the Cullercoats Volunteer Life Brigade on the same spot where the old wall was – but it was also realised that the village folk would still gather at the traditional place to watch how events would unfurl in times of great peril for the fishermen and that more than just a lifeboat house would be needed to manage any perilous situation.

So plans were drawn up for a building with a look-out tower which was completed and opened in 1879. The look-out tower was part of the clock turret, which also contained a bell that could also be rung in foggy conditions to guide the fishermen in their cobles back to the shore. The Cullercoats Volunteer Life Brigade which used the Watch House was formed in 1865 and was only the second such brigade to form in Britain.

When the Watch Tower was complete it had installed, 'one of the most approved American stoves, with all needful cooking utensils'. In the most severe of storms members of the Brigade would keep watch with the Coast Guard for vessels in distress, so assistance was almost instant and rescue chances greatly enhanced. This was when the value of the stove would come to the fore, giving hot food and warmth to those rescued who would have been cold, soaked and weak. The first caretaker and cleaner was a Mrs Susan Storey, the widow of a fisherman who had been drowned some years before.

A couple talk in the doorway of Sparrow Hall in around 1900.

The Watch Tower and lifeboat station, a popular gathering place for locals.

The choir in their Sunday best, ready for rehearsals.

An artist's impression of Sparrow Hall in its heyday.

The newly opened Fishermen's Mission, ready for its first service.

Laying the foundation stone for the new Fishermen's Mission.

The whole community turn out for the stone-laying ceremony at the Mission.

Above: The mission banner is paraded on the street, with musical accompaniment.

Left: Important members of the fishing community including Albert Lisle, B. Taylor and John Donkin. Albert is holding the accordion.

Opposite above: The Fishermen's Mission choir with the girls in their striking dresses.

Opposite below: Albert Lisle with young helpers working for the Mission.

Stout lads all: the Cullercoats Male choir.

Hat's the way to do it! Everyone has their headgear on a Mission trip to Warkworth in 1914.

three

Winslow
Homer

An artists' community grew in Cullercoats where painters such as H.H. Emmerson, Birket, Foster and J.D. Watson were inspired by both the fishermen and their constant battle with the North Sea and the fisherwomen who not only supported the men, but often put their own lives at risk in helping them either launch or return to shore.

By far the most famous of the painters to visit Cullercoats was American artist Winslow Homer. Homer had made his name as a frontline artist in the American Civil War, ignoring the flamboyant and heroic images of other painters for the realism of death, hunger and the solitude of the soldier. When he came to Europe in 1881 he didn't head for Paris, as was the fashion then, but came to the small fishing village of Cullercoats.

The fisherwomen became a constant source of inspiration to Homer during his stay. He admired their strength and endurance; he endowed them with a sense of calm dignity and grace. 'Sparrow Hall', one of only a few finished oil paintings produced in Cullercoats, shows women knitting or darning near the entrance to a seventeenth-century cottage, the oldest house in the village. The children among an array of barrels, baskets, crates, and floats scattered about the scene serve as reminders of the women's innumerable responsibilities: keeping house, tending children, repairing nets, gathering bait, and cleaning fish.

Sitting on the steps, a girl protectively helps a little child who dangles a bit of blue yarn in front of a cat. The 'Sparrow Hall' canvas is superbly painted and stands very high among his Cullercoats works, and indeed among Homer's images from any period.

Homer's Cullercoats women have often been called heroic, and, although he may have idealised them somewhat, the stern facts of their lives clearly instilled in them great strength and courage. Popular literature of the period depicted the fisherwomen of the North Sea region as uninhibited beauties who exemplified morality and intellectual honesty, a fitting subject for a high and profound art based on contemporary life. Homer remarked, 'There were none like them in my country.'

This page and opposite: Three watercolours by American artist Winslow Homer showing differing aspects of life for the Cullercoats fishing community.

Above and below: Two more of Winslow Homer's paintings showing how the fisherwomen appeared to the American artist: the painting above shows girls awaiting the return of their menfolk and, below, portrays the grace of one of the women Homer described as being 'different from any in America'.

Above: Waves crash against the rocks below Cliff House, on Cliff Row, in Cullercoats. It was said that a secret tunnel led from the house down to the rocks by the sea and was used to smuggle in contraband.

Below: The fisherwomen of Winslow Homer.

Above: The famous John Charlton painting 'The Women', showing the women of Cullercoats pulling the lifeboat *Percy* overland on its way to the aid of the *Lovely Nellie*.

Left: Another artist who worked extensively at Cullercoats, Henry Hetherington Emmerson. Born in Chester-le-Street, Emmerson came to Newcastle at the age of thirteen to study at the Government School of Design. He spent time in Paris and then London at the Royal Academy before coming back north in 1856, living briefly in Whickham, Ebchester and Stocksfield before moving to Cullercoats in 1865, where he kept a home until he died in 1895.

Right: These fishwives would have been mending their husband's nets.

Below: Homer's painting of a scene at Sparrow Hall. This is where the fisherwomen traditionally waited for their menfolk to return home from the sea.

Winslow Homer loved the power of the sea, the strength of the coble and the proud bearing of the fisherwomen.

No. 12 Bank Top, where the American artist lived while in Cullercoats.

four

The Richard
Silver Oliver

In 1937 Cullercoats received its first motor lifeboat, the single-engined *Richard Silver Oliver*. But lifeboats themselves weren't immune from tragedy, as was proven in April 1939 when the *Richard Silver Oliver* was overwhelmed by a freak wave while on a training exercise. Six of the ten men aboard were drowned.

She had set out at 2 p.m. on 22 April 1939 and was steering through a moderate north-westerly gale, northwards, towards St Mary's Island. The lifeboat then turned towards the shore. The *Richard Silver Oliver* was around 300 yards off Sharpness Point when an exceptionally heavy wave was observed heading towards her. The coxswain, Brunton, put the helm hard over, but it was too late: before the boat turned into the wave it broke over her full length and she was instantly capsized. This happened just before 3 p.m. and the stricken lifeboat began to drift towards the shore.

Jacob Brunton, the bowman, was thrown into the sea as the boat overturned and he managed to struggle onto the beach. John Smith, the district engineer, was trapped beneath the upturned hull. He swam out from under and climbed onto the bottom of the boat. Twice he was washed off into the sea before he decided his only hope was striking out for the shore, which he managed to reach before collapsing into unconsciousness.

Two crew members, James Carmichael and Oliver Tweedy, had also been trapped under the hull, but swam clear and clung to the upturned boat until it eventually washed ashore in King Edward's Bay. By the time the emergency services had arrived it was all over because the six who died had been washed ashore. Those who perished were Coxswain George Brunton, Second Coxswain Redford Armstrong, Motor Mechanic Leonard Abel, Assistant Mechanic John Heddon Scott, Station Honorary Secretary Lt-Commander Lionel Blakeney-Booth and his sixteen-year-old stepson, Naval Cadet Kenneth Biggar.

Despite the tragedy the lifeboat itself suffered only superficial damage and, after being righted on the beach, returned to Cullercoats under its own power. Although a new crew quickly stepped forward the lifeboat station had to be temporarily closed, because they refused to have a non-righting lifeboat again. The *Richard Silver Oliver* was replaced by the *Westmorland* in February 1940. The *Westmorland* served throughout the Second World War and until 1951, saving ninety-five lives.

A hot day at Cullercoats, with children in their bathing costumes beside one of the fishing cobles.

Fishermen discuss the day's fishing as they busy themselves in their cobles.

Villagers gather
sea coal.

Cobles bob about in the harbour as fishermen sort out their nets and bathers plodge on the water's edge.

Children, with creel and lobster pot, play on the rocks. The lad looks to be wearing an over-sized pair of waders.

The McCulley family with their coble.

Left: Henry 'Rough-it' Brown mends his nets as his grandsons, Billy and Tommy, look on. This picture was taken in Cullercoats in 1910. Henry may also have been known as 'Harry the Buck'.

Below: Cliff Row, in Cullercoats, overlooking Jakey's Beach, in 1905.

Opposite above: Men work away making their coble ready for a day's fishing.

Opposite below: Looking back at the bay from offshore.

Cobles packed tightly on the beach some time before 1900.

Looking out from Cullercoats at sunset.

Above: Fishermen returning with their baskets and catch after a fishing expedition.

Below: George Brunton with his coble.

Two fishwives wait with empty creels for their menfolk to bring the catch in.

Fishermen are ready to negotiate their coble onto a carriage to bring it up the beach.

five

Robert 'Scraper' Smith

Cullercoats lifeboat Coxswain Robert Smith was an inspirational figure among lifeboatmen and a welcome sight for sailors in distress when, with his small band of brave men, he came to their rescue. Many of his rescues are legendary, including ships such as the *Dunelm*, *Rohilla* and the *Bessheim*. It was 13 January 1913 when the SS *Dunelm* ran aground near Blyth in a raging storm. The seas were so strong that many of 'Scraper' Smith's crew refused to risk the ten-mile trip through the terrible seas. But 'Scraper' and five of his men felt they were honour-bound and set out on their rescue attempt in the *Henry Vernon*. They battled for an hour against the tempest before they reached the *Dunelm* with her crew clinging for dear life to the rigging.

Through the skill of 'Scraper' they saved every member of the crew but on the return journey a huge wave hit the boat and 'Scraper' was knocked unconscious after hitting the deck and fracturing several ribs. In this instance it was the skill of his well-trained crew which brought the lifeboat safely into Cullercoats harbour.

On 1 November 1916, the Norwegian steamer *Bessheim* was being blown onto the rocks in the River Tyne. Smith and his men made three perilous journeys and saved 118 passengers and crew. The King of Norway presented him with a silver cup in recognition of his and the crew's bravery.

On 30 October 1914 the hospital ship *Rohilla* had been driven onto a reef off Whitby. Local lifeboats were unable to reach the ship because of the massive waves and the only hope was a motor-driven lifeboat. Without a second's thought, 'Scraper' and his men set out in the *Henry Vernon* on a fifty-mile perilous journey through storm-tossed seas to come to the aid of the stricken ship.

It was a tremendous struggle for the crew just to keep the lifeboat on course, but eight hours later they put into Whitby to take stock before immediately setting out on their rescue mission. By then they were being watched by a massive crowd on the cliff tops who saw the little lifeboat frequently disappear into the large troughs, only to reappear again heading for the *Rohilla*.

'Scraper' took the *Henry Vernon* past the ship, before stopping and discharging gallons of oil over the boiling seas, which had the remarkable effect of flattening the waves. He turned the *Henry Vernon* and raced at full speed past the stern of the *Rohilla* and then guided the lifeboat with great skill towards the ship. A great cheer went up as the craft came together, but time was short as the sea was getting its strength back again.

Every one of the crew, more than forty men, scrambled onto the lifeboat which then started back to shore. Even then she was hit broadside by gigantic waves – but nothing could stop 'Scraper' and his men getting back to harbour. 'Scraper' became harbour master at Cullercoats and is said to have saved at least eight people from drowning in his small boat. As for his nickname of 'Scraper', nobody knows how he got it. It is thought maybe it was to do with scraping the bottom of the boats and because many in the village had the same name they were all given nicknames. This chapter focuses on the lifeboat service in Cullercoats, but Robert himself can be seen on pages 96 and 97.

Co-operator No. 1 and her crew set out on an exercise on harbour day.

The same lifeboat about to be put into the bay as crowds waving flags enjoy the spectacle.

The *Co-operator No. 2* being launched. Rescue was hazardous in the old 'pullers', lifeboats powered by oarsmen. Life and death depended on the strength of the oarsmen and their oars.

Here we see Coxswain Andrew Taylor instructing the crew of the *Co-operator No. 2*. There were so many Andrew Taylors in Cullercoats that they were known by nicknames.

Large crowds gather in Cullercoats Bay on Harbour Day.

During the day's ceremonies fishermen stand offshore in their cobles.

Above and below: Every year residents from all over Tyneside, in their Sunday best, turned out to give their support on Lifeboat Day helping to keep the funds coming in.

Cullercoats celebrates Lifeboat Saturday, many of the villagers carrying their replica lifeboats. You can also see the young girls with their small creels.

The lifeboatmen mingle with the crowd.

A military band, followed by a large crowd, marches through Front Street in 1922 playing pipes and drums.

As part of the ceremony the lifeboat itself is pulled up the bank from the lifeboat station.

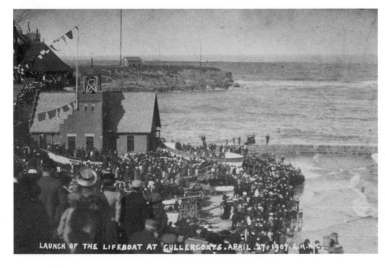

Lifeboat Day at Cullercoats in 1907 and large crowds gather for the launch of the lifeboat.

Cullercoats is thronged with visitors for Lifeboat Saturday.

Bedecked with flags flying in the wind, the lifeboat continues its journey through the streets on Lifeboat Day.

It is hauled from the sea after the lifeboatmen's training exercise.

The *Isaac and Mary Bolton*, on its carriage. Despite the caterpillar contraption you can still see people pulling the lifeboat.

The crew pose in front of their lifeboat.

Above and below: It's not a job for the weak or faint-hearted. A lifeboat is much heavier than the normal coble and it takes expert handling to get it from the sea onto its carriage, and then to and from the station.

A lifeboat goes off to the rescue.

The *Richard Silver Oliver* after it had been righted following the tragedy in 1939 which cost six lives.

The upturned *Richard Silver Oliver* being towed back to harbour.

Cullercoats fishermen discuss the tragedy.

The lifeboat is beached in King Edward's Bay and an injured lifeboatman is being carried up the stairs on a stretcher.

Shocked villagers gather around the craft.

The bodies of the dead men lie in the local church.

Men of Cullercoats turned out in force for the funeral procession in 1927 of Mr Robert ('Scraper') Smith, hero of the lifeboat service, who was awarded the RNLI gold medal — the lifeboat VC — for gallantry for his part in the rescue of survivors of the hospital ship, Rohilla, sunk in 1914. He was twice awarded the silver medal, made an OBE in 1924 and was coxwain of Tynemouth lifeboat for ten years, and a lifeboatman for 50 years. Among those identified in the procession as it passes Dial House are Jack Lisle, George Lisle, George Smith, William Taylor, Bart Taylor, Bob Scott, John Taylor, George Taylor, Martin Laidler, Jake Brunton, Bob Taylor, Peter Armstrong and Hedden Taylor.

Funeral of lifeboat VC hero

Above: Pictured in the *Evening Chronicle*, the funeral of Coxswain George Brunton, one of six who perished when the *Richard Silver Oliver* capsized during a training exercise in 1939.

Opposite above: The men of Cullercoats turn out in force for the funeral of lifeboat hero Coxswain Robert 'Scraper' Smith, in 1927. He was awarded the RNLI gold medal for gallantry – the lifeboat VC – for his actions in the rescue of survivors of the *Rohilla* hospital ship, sunk in 1914. He was twice awarded the silver medal and made an OBE in 1924.

Opposite below: The *Richard Silver Oliver* being hauled ashore after the tragedy.

CULLERCOTES FISHWIVES TRIP TO BLACKPOOL AUG. 4th. 1928.

The umbrellas are up but everyone is smiling as the Cullercoats fishwives take a trip to Blackpool in 1928.

'Thou shalt not pass' – unless you give a donation! Fishwives form a line across the road, determined, albeit in a friendly manner, to add to the lifeboat collection.

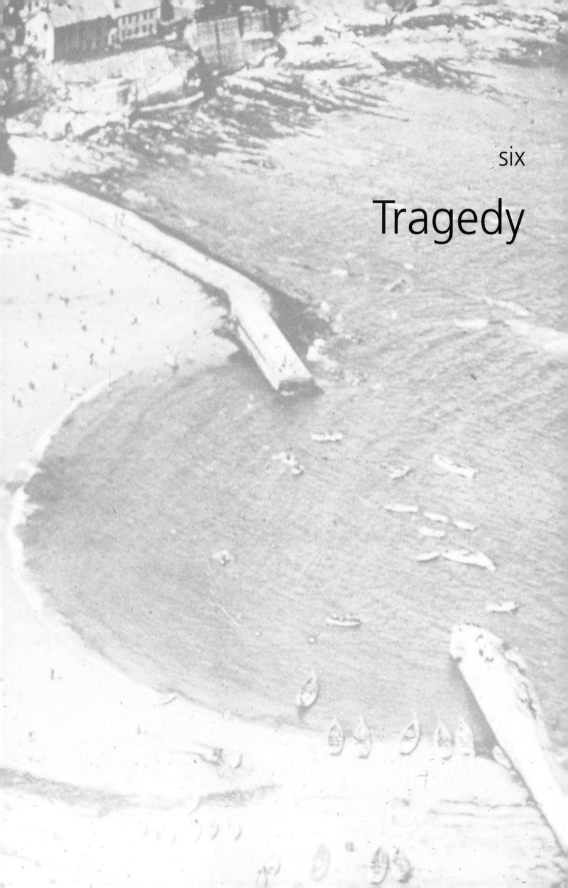

six

Tragedy

In 1848 Cullercoats suffered a massive tragedy when seven local men were drowned after a coble capsized in buffeting winds and high seas. A number of ships had been waiting offshore for pilots when the coble put out from Cullercoats carrying two fishermen and five river pilots.

The coble had just cleared the broken water when it was completely swamped by a wave. The crew had all just got to their feet when the coble was hit by a second large wave which turned the coble over.

Two of the men had disappeared but the other five were trying to hang on to the bottom of the coble. By this time the alarm had been raised on the shore and soon all the inhabitants of Cullercoats were at the shoreline. More cobles were launched in a rescue attempt but they were driven so strongly southward, away from the unfolding tragedy, that they had no chance of reaching any of the men hanging on to the upturned coble.

As each wave hit the coble it turned over and over and soon three more men had disappeared, leaving only two able to hang on. One had apparently lashed himself to the mast and was also holding on to the floating oars, but his strength was waning and soon he was overcome by the sea and perished.

The final ill-fated crew member, believed to be James Stocks, was known as a strong swimmer and although he was washed off the bottom of the coble a number of times he seemed always able to get back onto it. Finally, he was observed sitting on the coble, stripping off his jacket and waistcoat and preparing to swim ashore. The coble by this time was close to the rocks and Stocks' brother shouted to him: 'Jim, swim ashore.' Stock replied: 'I'm done, I'm done.' Although he made a great effort to reach the shore he eventually sunk below the sea. The men who drowned were brothers George and Robert Lisle; their sons Robert and George; Robert Clarke, who was a brother-in-law of the first mentioned George Lisle; James Stocks and Charles Pearson.

Another tragedy of the situation is that the wives and children of the doomed men were watching events unfurl from the shore. It was said that six wives and fourteen children under eleven years of age were left fatherless.

A large collection was gathered on their behalf and the Duke of Northumberland, who owned much of the land around Cullercoats, was deeply affected by the accident and provided funds so that the RNLI could establish a lifeboat station at Cullercoats.

An aerial view of a busy day at Cullercoats Bay.

Mr and Mrs Davie Taylor, and dogs, relax outside their home with a young member of their family.

The old Front Street in Cullercoats.

The grocer's shop in Station Road, which later became the Lloyds TSB Bank.

Judging by the short shadows, this picture was taken around midday in Huddleston Street.

Shops begin to open and people begin to talk as the day gets underway in Front Street, 1920.

The community turns out in force as a fire rages through St Margaret's church in 1903.

Opposite above: George Lisle talks to Princess Marina in a break during a royal visit to Cullercoats.

Opposite below: Local celebrity Polly Donkin is chaired through the streets by the people of Cullercoats.

'Happy to see you' – fishwife Nanny Gallon chats to the Duke of Kent on his Cullercoats visit.

The white Fisher Cottages in Front Street, Cullercoats.

J. Stocks and George Scott take their nets down to the cobles.

The Lucky Lukey Band of *Sunday Sun* readers, or they could have been the bearded wonders!

A family picture taken outside the White Cottages, on Back Row.

Brown's buildings, where many of the fisherfolk lived.

Fisherman John Taylor, with his magnificent beard, and his wife.

Above: Fishermen discharge their day's catch.

Left: Is it a monster? Crowds gather around the 11ft fish caught off Marsden and displayed on North Shields Fish Quay by George and John Taylor of Cullercoats.

Opposite, above and below: Two pictures showing a quiet Victorian day at Bank Top. The tramlines give evidence of a regular service from places such as Newcastle.

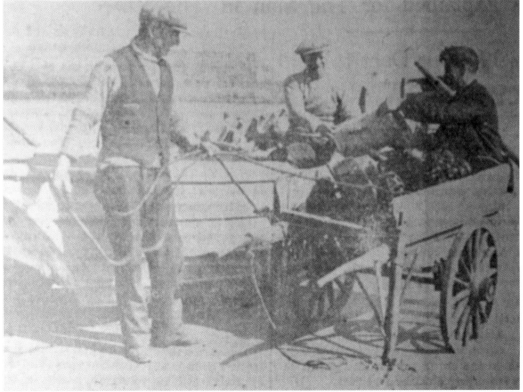

Edwardian Cullercoats; a horse and cart full of wares stands outside a shop next to the Ship Inn.

Building workers at Cullercoats.

Cobles lie in the sand of Cullercoats Bay after a long day's fishing, in the year 1895.

Sightseers visit the wreck of the *Fairymaid* as it lies on the beach.

Above: Fishwives and children, some in fancy dress, outside the Watch House.

Left: Gentlemen and ladies relax in the sun outside the Watch House.

Above: The nets are made ready, everything is checked and soon this little coble will be out at sea, chasing its daily catch.

Right: Fishermen show off part of their impressive haul.

Below: The fish shop in Station Road in Victorian times

Above: A gathering of female members of the Fishermen's Mission.

Left: Well-known local character Bolam Dick makes sure his nets are in good condition for the next day's fishing.

seven

Polly Donkin

Polly Donkin achieved almost national recognition as the Cullercoats fishwife who had been received by royalty and who could claim the friendship of titled families. Certainly her motherly figure, with its traditional costume, was one of the best known in the North East in her time.

Polly was born Mary Jane Shuttleworth in 1854 and, in her lifetime, raised over £1,000 for the Cullercoats lifeboat appeal, a vast sum in those times especially in a region where money was so scarce. But why was she called Polly? 'Aa cannot tell ye hoo Aa got it,' she once said. 'But I nivvor gat nothin' else. Me muther caaled us Polly. Constant Polly. An' me man nivvor gov us onny uther. Aa hev a niece called Isabella an' she gets nowt but Cissie. Aa divvent knaa hoo we get these names. But there it is, ye see. For shortness, mebbies.'

She married John Donkin on the 8 December 1878, but after eight days of snow and deep rifts she never thought she'd make it from Cullercoats to the little Methodist Chapel, in North Shields. It was still snowing when the only horse and cab in Cullercoats appeared in great distress at the bride's home. The driver said, 'Aa doot wor not gan te get te Sheels the day.' One horse, he went on, could never get through. However, he disappeared and returned with another and, in double harness, the team succeeded in pulling the cab through the drifts to the chapel and back. 'It was a varry stormy day,' Polly later recalled. 'But we've had plenty of sunshine since then. Happy days.'

Polly carried her creel of fish for sixty-one years. 'Aa went wi' the creel when Aa was a lassie o' siventeen. An Aa carried it until Aa was siventy-eight.' At first it was a small creel – 'Aboot three stone o' fish it held,' she said. 'An Aa carried it fr' heor te Sheels. Made a rest for me creel at the tornstiles as Aa went through the fields. There was ne traalers then, ya knaa.'

Later she got a full-sized creel. 'An' the full weight,' she added. 'Up to five stone o' fish in the creel, the white-handled bucket atop o' that, filled wi' fish, an' sumtimes an extra basket i' me hand.' By that time Polly was carrying her own weight in fish. 'Aa could elways de that,' said Polly. Later her musical cry, 'Will ye buy onny feesh?' was heard in Newcastle.

It was on this round that she was once attacked and robbed by two men as she walked along the railway from Friarside to Lintz Green station. One of her attackers came suddenly from behind a railway truck standing in a siding, and knocked her down; breaking her spectacles and cutting her face, before running off with her day's takings. This did not deter Polly from making the round again.

She was invited to London in 1931 to receive the gold brooch of the Royal National Lifeboat Institution from the Prince of Wales. After curtseying in front of the Prince, Polly was heard to say: 'God bless ye! Ye're a canny lad. Ivverybody in the North Country is axin' verry kindlie eftor ye, an' they hope ye'll not be lang in cummin back te Newcassel.'

Polly and John Donkin had three children. She died at the age of ninety-three in 1951.

Mrs M. Brunton (an axe at her feet), obviously getting on in years, surveys the scene.

Cullercoats fisherwoman Elizabeth Taylor puts her hand to her mouth to shout for customers.

Fisherwomen ready to head off on their rounds, carrying creels and selling the fish.

Creels full – these young fishwives look to be ready to take their fish to their customers.

They've had a little natter: all they need now is the cobles to come in and they can fill up their creels with fish and embark on their travels.

Fisherwomen young and old, in their fancy aprons and overdresses.

Three of the Cullercoats fisherwomen have a good gossip about the day's events.

Well-known fishwife Nanny Lisle poses with her creels.

Fishwives Mrs Storey and Polly Lisle.

A group of fisherwomen on a day's outing.

A young fisherwoman cleaning and selling crabs, *c.* 1930.

Happy fisherwomen, waiting on the beach, pose with their empty creels.

Above: They look to be at an age when carrying creels full of fish should have been far behind them, but these ladies walked miles carrying the day's catch.

Left: These Cullercoats fishwives are still doing their rounds during the Second World War, as you can see by the cardboard boxes which contained gas masks. They have overcome the minor difficulties of everyday travel and still pretty well keep to their original rounds.

eight

Cliff House

Probably Cullercoats' most intriguing property is Cliff House. It is positioned on the cliff top (hence its name), overlooking the sea and has a history of being heavily involved in the smuggling trade.

The property was probably built by Thomas Armstrong, who was 'commander of His Majesty's cutter, *Bridlington*'. The story goes that he had engineered the dismissal of the previous captain and been appointed in his place. The *Bridlington* was a customs vessel that patrolled the seas from Newcastle to Sunderland, with the job of intercepting smugglers going about their business. But as is sometimes the way, Thomas Armstrong himself was thought to be in league with the local smugglers. He ruled his ship, the *Bridlington*, with a rod of iron but, in 1771, he was suspended from duty for letting smugglers escape. It is believed he had helped them escape.

Although he eventually returned to duty, the full story of his complicity emerged. In 1776, Lucas and Wallard, two notorious smugglers, were seen and the authorities tipped off. Armstrong and his men were ordered to arrest them. Lucas and Wallard were taken but strangely allowed to walk at leisure on deck between the three ships and seemed on unusually good terms with the officers. Not unnaturally, the smugglers soon made their getaway by commandeering a rowing boat. The ensuing verdict on Armstrong was damning; he was found to have been in great breach of duty, instrumental in their escape and of giving a false account of goods seized. He was dismissed from duty. He had been under investigation on at least five other charges.

It was said that it was because of his collusion with smugglers that Armstrong could afford to build such a grand house as Cliff House, but that it not the end of the story, because it also sheds light on some of the bizarre architectural features of Cliff House which include a secret cellar found underneath the floor of Armstrong's study. This leads to a tunnel which in those days would have run down through the cliffs onto the beach below. The cellar also had cages in which to hold prisoners.

The fishing coble *Europe* is brought up from the sea on its carriage.

Cobles and carriages litter the beach, left high and dry by the tide.

The *Richard Silver Oliver* lifeboat is taken on a training run, under full sail, across the bay.

The old-fashioned way – a coble, probably going for repair, is hauled up the bank and away from the beachfront by a team of men.

Above: 'Scraper' displays a chest-full of shining medals.

Opposite above: Coxswain Robert 'Scraper' Smith, in the centre of the picture after being presented with his medal at Buckingham Palace.

Opposite below: Posing for a picture with the fisherwomen.

Above: Another typical harbour scene, with cobles moored after a day's fishing.

Left: Fishermen fill bags with sand to act as ballast on their coble.

Above: Cobles
viewed from the
southside of the
harbour. They
have not long
returned from a
day's fishing.

Right: The
lifeboat *Sir James
Knott.*

Left: The indomitable Polly Donkin showing off the fish she has for sale.

Below: Polly Donkin, on her stall, collecting for Lifeboat Day.

nine

Wreck of the Lovely Nellie

The 1904 painting 'The Women', by artist John Charlton (see page 34), illustrates a dramatic scene which shows the women of Cullercoats dragging the lifeboat *Percy* over the headland, in the teeth of a blizzard, to launch it near the stricken ship *Lovely Nellie*. On New Year's Day, in 1861, the *Lovely Nellie*, a brig from Seaham, was seen by the coastguards stationed at the Spanish Battery, at Tynemouth, going onto the rocks. She was deeply laden with cargo and struggling in vain to get northwards, away from the danger. She put up a distress flag and was looking doomed when the Cullercoats lifeboat was called out.

By then the cliffs were lined with crowds of onlookers fearing the worst for the stricken ship. The *Lovely Nellie* had lost most of her sails and with the heavy seas breaking around her she was proving uncontrollable. She was now in the hands of the elements. The crew grabbed one last chance and ran her for Whitley Sands but with her heavy cargo she struck sunken rocks while still three-quarters of a mile off the shore. She was too far away from the rockets and line and the only hope for the crew was the Cullercoats lifeboat.

The truth of the painting is not known, but through the driving rain and wind, lifeboatmen, fishermen and fisherwomen, with the help of six horses, dragged the boat, on a carriage, to the sea shore. The crew, showing their strength with the oars, soon reached the ship, which had the crew clinging for their lives to the rigging with waves breaking over her half-mast high. With skill and courage the men of Cullercoats brought their boat alongside the vessel and secured it with grapples while the stricken sailors scrambled aboard from the rigging. But even then three were swept into the sea. Two were quickly picked up and the third was rescued with a 'grasp of iron' in his last seconds of life.

But as the lifeboat was pulling away to safety a young cabin boy was observed on the deck crying for help. He was wounded in the head and blood poured down his face. The lifeboatmen tried to entice him to jump out of the rigging but fear kept his grip tight. They dashed in time and again, but the lad was too fearful to attempt to leap the gap. Eventually the main mast was about to fall where the lifeboat was and with everyone growing pale, clenching teeth and shedding tears, they had to pull away. This they did just in time, as one minute more beside the ship would have brought disaster for the lifeboat and everyone in her. A hoarse voice yelled 'cut the rope' and the boats parted as the *Lovely Nellie* broke up. The boy, his face bloodied and tearful, fell into the sea. As he brought his hands out of the sea the lifeboat rushed to him, but too late: when they reached the spot he had disappeared. Little Tommy was the only casualty that terrible night.

The bottom of Eskdale Terrace before the Fishermen's Mission was built.

Everything is set up for the Harvest Festival at the Fishermen's Mission.

Above: A typical Victorian scene at Bank Top with visitors to Cullercoats enjoying the sea air.

Below: Front Street, around 1895.

Above: A typical picture of what happens when a fishing coble arrives back – there are plenty of willing hands to haul it ashore.

Below: Coast Guard drill. The men are firing off a rocket, which would be used to take a line to a stricken ship.

This fishwife posing by the rocks shows just what Homer saw in these hard-working and proud women of Cullercoats.

Cobbled floor, wooden barrels, old steps and wooden banister – this was known as Nancy's Yard, but could that be Nancy climbing the stairs?

George and Lisle Brunton with their father and another relative.

Cullercoats girls collecting for Lifeboat Day.

Above: Men of Cullercoats hauling a coble up the beach.

Right: A fisherman setting his bait, ready to set out for the day's fishing.

Left: Mr and Mrs Storey check their catch of crabs and lobsters outside their home.

Below: Cullercoats residents pictured on Lifeboat Day, in front of the town's lifeboat.

Albert Lisle and family pose for a picture.

A stallholder tries to tempt a local VIP with her wares as she raises money for the lifeboat appeal.

Fisherwoman Maggie Bolam at her stall on Harbour Day.

George Lisle plays the accordion at a Cullercoats civic ceremony.

John Lisle and family sitting for the camera.

Members of the Watch House.

Four faded but rare pictures which show the extent of the flood that gripped Cullercoats in 1910: three amused children stand by the partly submerged tracks; a train is stuck in the station; the flooded platforms; the floods reach Eskdale Terrace.

Dressed in her Sunday best, this lady has probably retired from her days of carrying heavy creels.

The crew of the coble *Elizabeth* after bringing her ashore on her carriage.

A trip leaving the Watch House for a day somewhere in Northumberland.

A church parade leads the way in the Blessing of the Boats ceremony at Cullercoats.

The cliffs of Tynemouth, where many a rescue took place.

Right: One of the distinguished lifeboat couples,
Mr and Mrs Taylor.

Below: The Ship Hotel, once popular with local
fishermen.

The Ship Hotel overlooks the back of the Fisher Cottages.

A quiet day by the sea.

The lifeboat house and Watch Tower.

A very faded but lovely image of Edwardian youngsters on a day out at the seaside.

One of the old ladies of the village, who has done her stint as a fishwife and now looks after her grandchild.

It's party time as villagers dress up in fancy dress.

A local dignitary talks to the former fisherfolk at a garden party in around 1900.

With a full creel, this tough-looking fisherwoman is ready to set off on her round.

Mrs Storey, hands on hips, in a classic fishwife pose for a studio photograph.

A fishwife, watched by a colleague, takes up a saucy pose for the camera.

A fishwife poses for a studio picture. Her clothes are all freshly cleaned and creels spotless.

Other local titles published by Tempus

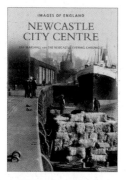

Newcastle West End
RAY MARSHALL AND THE EVENING CHRONICLE

This superb collection of photographs from the *Newcastle Evening Chronicle*'s picture library gives a fascinating insight into the life of the people and the changes they experienced in the West End of Newcastle during the last century. With rare images of celebrations and disasters, institutions such as Armstrong's works and the great clearances of the 1960s and 1970s, it offers a unique and nostalgic glimpse into the city's past.

978 0 7524 3351 6

Newcastle City Centre
RAY MARSHALL AND THE EVENING CHRONICLE

This book continues Ray Marshall's best-selling series of archive photographs of Newcastle. From workmen putting the finishing touches to the Tyne Bridge in the 1920s – without a harness or safety helmet in sight – and dockers at work to landmarks such as Bessie Surtees House and the locals quite literally fighting to get into the Christmas sales, this is an indepth pictorial history of the city which will delight all who know the area.

978 07524 3998 3

Newcastle Ragged School
WENDY PRAHMS

This is the complete history of Newcastle Ragged School. Containing everything from the annual reports of the school – many of which shocked the nation – to the history of the local Board Schools and other rival institutions, and illustrated with many rare archive images of Newcastle in centuries past, this is an indespensible guide to this near forgotten institution.

978 07524 4088 0

Sunderland Empire: a Centenary History
ALISTAIR ROBINSON

With more than a hundred images from the Empire's own collection, this is a fascinating, insightful and beautifully written history of Sunderland's very own Empire; from the days of mashers and male impersonators such as Vesta Tilley all the way through to the modern day, this book will delight all lovers of the theatre.

978 07524 4340 9

If you are interested in purchasing other books published by Tempus, or in case you have difficulty finding any Tempus books in your local bookshop, you can also place orders directly through our website

www.tempus-publishing.com